BIBLIOGRAPHY

Gastineau H. *North Wales Illustrated,* Republished by EP Publishing Ltd., 1977
Morris D.J. *The Snowdon Mountain Railway,* Ian Allan Ltd., 1960
Mulholland H. *Guide to Wales' 3000-foot Mountains,* Wirral, 1982
Ransome-Wallis P. *Snowdon Mountain Railway,* Ian Allan Ltd., 1969
Roscoe T. *Wanderings and Excursions in North Wales,* Republished by E.J. Morton, 1973
Rowland E.G. *The Ascent of Snowdon,* Cicerone Press, 1975
Styles S. *What to see in Beddgelert,* William H. Eastwood, Beddgelert 1972
Snowdon Summit, Snowdonia Press, Porthmadog
Walks in Snowdonia, Photo Precision Ltd

ACKNOWLEDGEMENTS

All the postcards in this book have been selected from the author's own collection.
Janet Penny of Beddgelert, for the loan of her valued copy of *What to see in Beddgelert* by Showell Styles, now out of print.
Frank Rhodes of Lightwood, for editing this book.
Gillian Jackson, for proof-reading.

iii

INTRODUCTION

The area of North Wales called Snowdonia was defined in the formation of the National Park in 1951 and covers 833 square miles. However, it is the smaller area of Snowdon and its immediate surroundings which is the subject of this book, together with a section dedicated to the Snowdon Mountain Railway.

All the fifteen 3000ft summits of Wales lie in this area, the highest being Yr Wyddfa at 3559ft. If you can picture an aerial view of a starfish and liken this to a mountain seen from above, you can visualise Snowdon, with its longest arm stretching out to Llanberis. Moving in a clockwise direction brings you to the first half of the Snowdon Horseshoe, and one of the finest ridge walks in the world, starting at the summit of Crib Goch, 3021ft and leading across to Crib-y-Ddysgl, 3493ft, before joining the Llanberis arm and reaching to the summit.

Within the Snowdon Horseshoe lie the lakes of Llyn Glaslyn and Llyn Llydaw, then comes the arm leading to Y Lliwedd, 2947ft, and the second half of the Horseshoe ridge walk. It is down this arm that the Watkin Path descends into Cwm-y-Llan and Nant Gwynant. The South Ridge, at the bottom of which is Yr Aran, 2451ft, is the steepest but shortest of the popular routes and is a real test for calf and thigh muscles. Finally comes the arm forming the south-west side of Cwm Clogwyn, carrying one of the oldest footpaths, The Snowdon Ranger, via Clogwyn d'ur Arddu.

Surrounding the Snowdon Massif are Llanberis and its Pass; the Glyders, beyond which can be found the A5 London to Holyhead road surveyed by Thomas Telford; Capel Curig and its twin lakes, Llynau Mymbyr; Moel Siabod; Moel Hebog, overlooking Beddgelert; Mynydd Mawr and the old Roman road leading to Segontium, on the River Seiont near Caernarfon.

Snowdonia is the name given to the area around Mount Snowdon, whose name probably originates from the Saxon word for a snow- covered hill. Eryri is the more romantic Welsh name, meaning 'abode of eagles'. However, the large birds seen there today are buzzards, the eagles having left for eyries new.

Climbing in this area is a relatively recent development, but the first men to have reached the summit of Snowdon would undoubtedly have been the Celts. Not for them the well-laid pathways, nor the summertime refreshments now available at the top.

Although Snowdon is the indisputable 'King of Mountains' in Wales, there are others to be climbed here, and valleys to be explored. All are steeped in history and legend.

Whatever your preference — ENJOY IT.

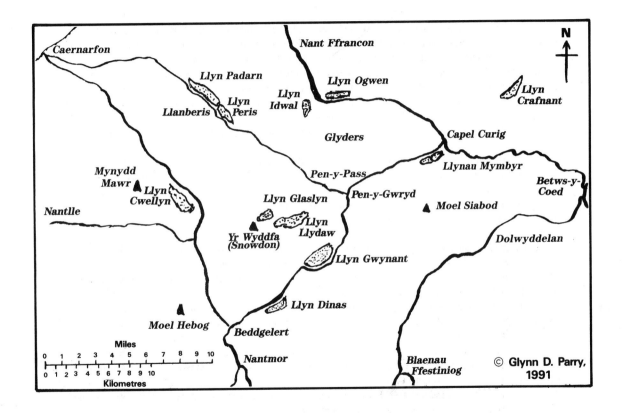

THE AUTHOR

Despite my name and the fact that I was born on St David's Day, I am not a Welshman. Along with thousands of his countrymen, my great grandfather moved from Caergybi (Holyhead) to Liverpool in the search for work. However, the affinity remains, since I feel very much at home in Wales, and nowhere more so than in the area around Snowdon.

Being a fair-weather walker, I spend time in the mountains from early spring to late autumn, always carrying my camera. In order to enjoy the full length of the day and to avoid the traffic, my wife and I rise at 5.30 a.m. on Sunday mornings and generally arrive at our destination around 8.15 a.m. to 8.30 a.m. Any later and you can forget the convenient car parks for Snowdon and the southern approach to the Glyders.

I came to mountain walking in my mid-forties, which was far too late in life; but perhaps we all regret not discovering our great pleasures much earlier.

One of my other hobbies is making slide presentations to local groups, societies and clubs; more than seventy being done in 1990. This combines well with my hobby of collecting old postcards, such as those in this book. I was a founder member of the Wirral Postcard Club, formed in 1987, with the club going from strength to strength, attracting good attendance each year. It is here that I have acquired the bulk of my postcard collection. Since every trip into North Wales results in colour transparencies being added to my library, it is natural to wish to see how the same places looked in earlier days, and thus expand on my knowledge and experience of the area.

Glynn D. Parry
Bromborough
Wirral

The Village, Bettws-y-Coed.

BETWS-Y-COED, c. 1905

Many people travelling into Snowdonia will use the A5 road through Betws-y-Coed (the Chapel in the Woods). During Victorian times the village was a popular resort with honeymooners. The woods to which the name refers were the natural broad-leaved areas, with trees like the oak, which had been cleared before the 1920s. They were replaced by trees not native to the area, mainly conifers. The card, published by Valentine's, shows Edwardian ladies and gentlemen near to a 'Post Card Palace' on the road leading out of Betws-y-Coed towards Capel Curig.

BETWS-Y-COED, c. 1922

The Tanlan Hotel and Restaurant opposite the road from the railway station. To the left is the Booking Office for Royal Red Motors and to the right is Betws-y-Coed Post Office. Although this is a Valentine's postcard from the 1920s the photographer has taken a view which includes the shop selling Judge's Postcards, seen just to the right of the Tanlan Restaurant. The church of Betws-y-Coed has a monument to Gruffydd, the son of Daffydd Goch, who died in the fourteenth century and was a son of Daffydd, brother of Llewellyn the Last, the last Prince of North Wales.

WATERLOO BRIDGE, BETWS-Y-COED, c. 1900

How many motorists, or their passengers, give consideration to the bridge carrying the A5 across the Afon Conwy, the confluence of the Afonau Conwy and Lledr? Known as the Waterloo Bridge, explained by the inscription thereon, it should impress upon the mind of all local schoolchildren the year in which the Battle of Waterloo was fought, 1815. This beautiful structure is of cast iron.

FAIRY GLEN BETTWS-Y-COED. (205).

FAIRY GLEN, NEAR BETWS-Y-COED, 1938

A slow shutter speed on the camera is the secret behind the impression of movement in the water on this card of the Fairy Glen. It is just off the A470 Llandudno to Cardiff road, on the Dolwyddelan side of the junction with the A5. It is the Afon Conwy, having been joined a little upstream by the Afon Machno, which tumbles through this great opening in the rocks. Over the centuries, the passage of water has worn holes in the stones in the river, creating the fantastic patterns to be seen.

Ugly House, Betws-y-Coed

THE UGLY HOUSE, NEAR BETWS-Y-COED

Ty Hyll (the Ugly House) lies on the A5 between Betws-y-Coed and Capel Curig, at the end of the bridge across the Afon Llugwy. Built in about 1475, it is of dry stone construction with extremely thick walls. Its age and condition are sufficient to indicate the strength of the building which has, as would be expected, a roof of slate.

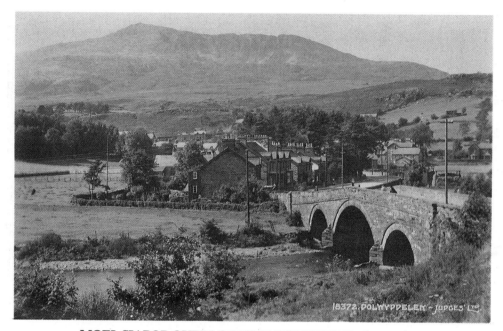

MOEL SIABOD OVERLOOKING DOLWYDDELAN, c. 1920

Running through Llanrwst, by-passing Betws-y-Coed and down the Lledr Valley to Blaenau Ffestiniog, the A470 gives a splendid view of Moel Siabod (Shepherds Mountain) 2861 ft. Two popular routes are used to reach the summit. A gentle grassy climb, through woodland on the lower slopes, starts from the side of Llyn Mymbyr at Capel Curig. For those who enjoy a challenge, the ridge on the Dolwyddelan side, starting from Llyn y Foel, is a little more taxing. Near to Dolwyddelan is the Castle which was built by the Welsh in the twelfth century to protect the road through the Lledr Valley. The English captured it in the thirteenth century. The card shows the view from near the railway, close to the bridge carrying the minor road across the Afon Lledr and up to the A470.

Crafnant Lake, Nr Trefriw.

LLYN CRAFNANT, c. 1902

A little-used pathway climbs gently from Capel Curig; having climbed the stile at the beginning and passed the chapel, the path turns gently right and through a small wood before emerging at the start of a slope leading, after several interesting turns, to a bird's-eye view of Llyn Crafnant. The area around here was used for lead mining and the resultant holes are filled with undrinkable water, unlike Llyn Crafnant and its neighbour Llyn Cowlyd which are used as reservoirs. During the late 1940s and early 1950s the farther shore of Llyn Crafnant was planted with pine saplings.

The plantation extended well up the hillside and was harvested from the 1980s onwards.

CAPEL CURIG, c. 1905

The village of Capel Curig is on the A5, mainly at the junction with the road through Nant Gwryd, the A4086. The ancient settlement named after Curig, son of Ilid, a seventh century Welsh saint, is almost two miles in length, with its houses and hotels stretched out over the distance. Overshadowed by Moel Siabod and its now disused quarries it has long been a centre for climbing and walking. This card, published by Photochrom in the Glossy Photo Series, shows part of the village behind which can be seen Clogwyn Mawr and, in the extreme distance, Craig Wen, 1770 ft, which overlooks Llyn Crafnant.

4946. THE LAKES CAPEL CURIG.   JUDGES' LTD.

SNOWDON FROM CAPEL CURIG, c. 1920

Surely one of the classic views of Snowdon; taken from just above the Royal Hotel, Capel Curig, the view shows the twin lakes, Llynau Mymbyr and the Snowdon Massif. Yr Wyddfa, 3559 ft, is obscured by cloud, but clearly seen are the twin peaks of Y Lliwedd, the higher of them being 2947 ft and marking the approaching end to the Snowdon Ridge walk which commences at Crib Goch, 3021 ft. Crib Goch is seen to the right, without obscuring cloud, and is said to be the start of the finest ridge walk in Britain if not the world! The largest building in the foreground is now Plas-y-Brenin, reopened in 1955 as a centre for outdoor activities, including dry-slope skiing, but it was formerly...

The Royal Hotel, Capel-Curig

ROYAL HOTEL, CAPEL CURIG, c. 1910

…The Royal Hotel, built in 1804 to serve the travellers on the turnpike to Holyhead. Built by Lord Penrhyn, it lies alongside the road from Capel Curig to Pen-y-Gwryd. The former hotel is now owned by the Sports Council.

VIEW FROM ROYAL HOTEL, CAPEL CURIG, c. 1920

The view from the garden of the Royal Hotel is across Llyn Mymbyr with the lower slopes of the Glyders on the right and the well- known view of Snowdon, seen here snow-capped. Today the chances are that the lake would be dotted with canoes being used by those staying at Plas-y-Brenin. Much of the garden, seen here with daffodils in the early stage of spring growth, has disappeared beneath the dry-ski slope.

THE OGWEN VALLEY, c. 1905

It is through this valley and into Nant Ffrancon that Thomas Telford's fine London to Holyhead road, the A5, passes on its way between Capel Curig and Bethesda. Gradients no greater than 1 in 20 ensure a speedy passage for all vehicles. This road replaced earlier roads, the earliest being a Roman roadway still to be seen on the opposite side of the Afon Llugwy. The expansion of the slate industry at Penrhyn necessitated an improved road, which resulted in a turnpike through Nant Ffrancon and the Ogwen Valley, opening in 1805, and paid for by Richard Pennant, owner of Bethesda and Penrhyn Quarries. Ten years later Telford was to commence his road-building, which took a total of four years for this section. Tryfan is like a stegosaurus eating its way into the Glyders.

Llyn Idwal and the Devil's Kitchen, N. Wales.   Abrahams' Series. No. 51. Keswick.

CWM IDWAL, c. 1900

Cwm Idwal, with its placid Llyn Idwal, is overshadowed by the magnificence of the Devil's Kitchen, Twll-du (the Black Hole). The lake has a legend telling of Idwal, son of Owain Gwynedd, Prince of North Wales, who was thrown into the lake by his foster-father. Since that time no birds have flown over the waters. A thousand years ago this whole area would have presented a very different view, with great forests of broad-leaved trees and an abundance of wild life, including deer. Cwm Idwal became the first National Nature Reserve in Wales in 1954. An undated, unused card published in the Lake District!

13

41164. BANGOR: IDWAL LAKE, THE DEVIL'S KITCHEN.

TWLL-DU, c. 1900

Twll-du (the Black Hole) the Devil's Kitchen is a great vertical cleft in the rock above Cwm Idwal. Thomas Pennant, the Welsh-born writer and walker, who published the first worthwhile book on the mountains of Snowdonia, wrote of Twll-du, 'I ventured to look down to this dreadful aperture and found its horrors far from being lessened by my exalted situation.' That was in the eighteenth century, but in more recent times it has been described in climbers' terms as standing '...in a class by itself, not of severity but of character...'

Nant Ffrancon from Glyder Fach. 9139

NANT FFRANCON, c. 1930

The twin summits of the Glyders, Fach and Fawr, are connected by a wide plateau from which can be seen Snowdon across the Llanberis Pass. When climbing from Pen y Pass, the arrival at the summit reveals this breathtaking view down Nant Ffrancon. Llyn Bochlwyd with Llyn Ogwen are to the right, with Pen-yr-Ole Wen, 3211 ft, rising above. Through the Pass can be seen clearly the Afon Ogwen, which enters the sea near Penrhyn Castle. Also seen is the A5, to the right of the river; but for the old road you must look carefully to the opposite side of the valley.

TRYFAN AND THE GLYDERS, c. 1910

Prominent in the picture is Tryfan, 3010 ft, in this view of the road through Nant Ffrancon. Leaving the route of the A5 near Rhaeddr Ogwen, the old road built by the Romans takes the west side of the valley before rejoining the 'new' route at the end of Nant Ffrancon, but it is no better than a track. Telford's new road was a great improvement.

NANT FFRANCON PASS SHOWING TRYFAN.

TOP OF NANT FFRANCON, c. 1920

The top of Nant Ffrancon at the ends of Llyn Ogwen and Cwm Idwal. Prominent again is Tryfan in this view published in the 1920s. Nant Ffrancon, according to Henry Gastineau in his book *North Wales Illustrated,* first published in 1830, is a corruption of Nant yr Afanc (Valley of Beavers), supposedly denominated from having been formerly a covert for those amphibious animals, no longer inhabitants of the country, but found, according to report, in this valley ''less than a century ago.''

17

CAERNARFON CASTLE, c. 1918

In order to suppress the rebellious Welsh it was an English king, Edward I, who built a series of castles in the principality. Harlech, Conway and Caernarfon, built in 1283, were constructed at strategic points. All are magnificent examples of English castle, but it was at Caernarfon that King Edward I presented to the Welsh their first English Prince of Wales.

The card was postally used on 25 May 1918 and bears the message, 'Nellie, Don't forget to go to school on Monday.' Posted from Bangor, it was addressed to Nellie, c/o an address near to Todmorden in Lancashire!

THE CASTLE AND RIVER, CAERNARFON, c. 1900

The small harbour at Caernarfon is on the Afon Seiont, near the point where the river runs into Afon Menai (the Menai Strait). Caernarfon Castle was intended as the royal headquarters in Wales, following the English victory over the Welsh, who had been led by Prince Llewelyn of North Wales. On the left, in this view published by Valentines, is the mighty Eagle Tower with its three turrets and continuing the style of keep favoured by the Normans. Despite its size the castle could be defended by as few as one hundred soldiers.

Swing Bridge Carnarvon

ABER BRIDGE, CAERNARFON, c. 1911

Aber Bridge, the swing bridge across the entrance to the harbour on the Afon Seiont, is overlooked by the Eagle Tower of the Castle. The material used in the construction of Caernarfon Castle came partly from the old Roman fortress of Segontium, a limestone which was brought over from Ynys Mon (Anglesey). The Aber Bridge, seen in this card published by Stewart & Woolf and postally used in September 1911, has been replaced by a modern structure using the same basic principle as the original.

CASTLE SQUARE, CAERNARFON, c. 1902

The Queen's Gate, the top of which can just be seen to the right of the terrace of houses, is named after Queen Eleanor, wife of King Edward I, and is the place where the Prince of Wales, first son of the monarch, is presented to his people. The statue in the centre of the photograph is that of Sir Hugh Owen (1804-1881) who was a pioneer in education in North Wales.

CASTLE SQUARE AND TOWN, CAERNARFON, c. 1923

A view of Castle Square, Caernarfon, not from the Eagle Tower, which is at the other end of the Castle. There is a steam wagon in the centre of the square where in later years would be seen Crosville buses and also those of Whiteways of Beddgelert. The card was published by Valentines in the 'Autochrome' series in 1923, which was two years before Crosville began their first operations from Caernarfon.

WFR.24.

MAIN STREET AND ELEPHANT MOUNTAIN, WAENFAWR.

WAENFAWR, c. 1938

Waenfawr, on the Caernarfon to Beddgelert road, was where I remember spending one of my earliest holidays in North Wales. Each time we travelled to Caernarfon it was by Whiteways buses from Beddgelert, and one of those was an ex-Birkenhead Corporation Transport vehicle which had, at one time, plied the road where we lived in Wirral. Elephant Mountain, seen in the card, is Mynydd Mawr (the Big Mountain) 2290 ft, overlooking Llyn Cwellyn and giving from its summit a splendid view of Snowdon. The name Waenfawr means Great Meadow.

SNOWDON FROM NEAR PORTHMADOG, c. 1925

Another classic view of Snowdon as seen from Porthmadog. In the foreground is Traeth Mawr, the land reclaimed from the sea by William A. Maddocks' embankment built between 1807 and 1811 and known as 'The Cob'. Nantmor, which is further up the Glaslyn valley, gives an indication in its original name, of how much land has been reclaimed. Originally the area was called Nant-y-Mor (the Pass on the Sea). The mountain rising on the left is Moel Hebog, 2566 ft, which overlooks the village of Beddgelert.

SNOWDON FROM LLYN CWELLYN, c. 1920

It is here, on the side of Llyn Cwellyn, that possibly the oldest footpath up Snowdon begins its ascent. Early climbers would attempt an assault from the western side, generally from Beddgelert or from here, near Llyn Cwellyn, using the leadership of a local guide. John Morton, the innkeeper and guide, in the mid-nineteenth century, named his hostel after the title he had given himself: The Snowdon Ranger. The Snowdon Ranger Youth Hostel is adjacent to the similarly named footpath, which is an extremely pleasant climb — especially when coupled with the Rhyd Ddu Path for the descent.

Y-GARN (2089 FT.) & RHYD-DDU-VILLAGE.   OS3535

RHYD DDU c. 1945

Y-Garn, the second mountain in the area close to Snowdon to bear that name, is at the beginning of the Nantlle ridge walk. Y-Garn is at the head of Nant Ffrancon. The village school-house in Rhyd Ddu was the birthplace of the poet T.H. Parry-Williams (1887-1975). The Welsh Highland Railway, which closed in 1937, had a station at South Snowdon, near Rhyd Ddu, and its site is now used as a car park at the bottom of the Rhyd Ddu path up Snowdon. The road to Nantlle leaves the A4085 Beddgelert to Caernarfon road, here at the village called 'Black Ford', the crossing of the Afon Gwyrfai.

26

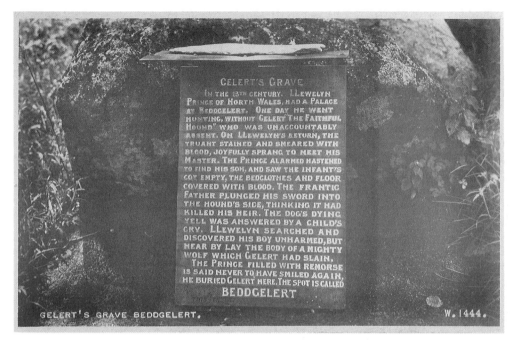

GELERT'S GRAVE

IN THE 13TH CENTURY, LLEWELYN
PRINCE OF NORTH WALES, HAD A PALACE
AT BEDDGELERT. ONE DAY HE WENT
HUNTING, WITHOUT GELERT "THE FAITHFUL
HOUND" WHO WAS UNACCOUNTABLY
ABSENT. ON LLEWELYN'S RETURN, THE
TRUANT STAINED AND SMEARED WITH
BLOOD, JOYFULLY SPRANG TO MEET HIS
MASTER. THE PRINCE ALARMED HASTENED
TO FIND HIS SON, AND SAW THE INFANT'S
COT EMPTY, THE BEDCLOTHES AND FLOOR
COVERED WITH BLOOD. THE FRANTIC
FATHER PLUNGED HIS SWORD INTO
THE HOUND'S SIDE, THINKING IT HAD
KILLED HIS HEIR. THE DOG'S DYING
YELL WAS ANSWERED BY A CHILD'S
CRY. LLEWELYN SEARCHED AND
DISCOVERED HIS BOY UNHARMED, BUT
NEAR BY LAY THE BODY OF A MIGHTY
WOLF WHICH GELERT HAD SLAIN.
THE PRINCE FILLED WITH REMORSE
IS SAID NEVER TO HAVE SMILED AGAIN,
HE BURIED GELERT HERE. THE SPOT IS CALLED
BEDDGELERT

GELERT'S GRAVE BEDDGELERT.   W. 1444.

GELERT'S GRAVE, c. 1930

Who can resist this emotional tale which has been told over the generations, and who would suggest that it is simply the invention of a local entrepreneur, a hotelier, who wanted to encourage visitors to the area many, many years ago? Did someone really witness the hotelier, and an assistant, carrying the original stone slab to this point?

GELERT'S GRAVE, c. 1900

Beddgelert (Gelert's Grave) lies near to the bank of the Afon Glaslyn and gives its name to the adjacent village. It is in a field, approached by a footpath from the village, that the grave of 'the faithful hound' can be found.

RIVER COLWYN, BEDDGELERT, c. 1910

Nestling on either side of both the Colwyn and the Glaslyn, the village of Beddgelert lies in a hollow overshadowed by mountains. The Afon Colwyn has its source on the western side of the Snowdon Massif. Passing what remains of the ancient Beddgelert Forest, it tumbles down Nant Colwyn adjacent to the old Roman road out of Segontium, until it enters Beddgelert and, having passed through the old bridge, joins the Afon Glaslyn on its way to Porthmadog.

29

BEDDGELERT, c. 1900

The road surface seen here can not be much better than when the first turnpike reached Beddgelert in 1805. Horseback at best, but more than likely on foot, was the mode of travel prior to that date, and when a Nicholas Owen arrived in Beddgelert in 1792 he wrote, '…the village ale house of Beddgelert, the place of rest nearest the bridge, affords no variety of accommodation; the catalogue of negatives is abundant. No butcher's meat, no wheaten bread, no wine, no spirits…' Oh dear! What a sad place; but had things changed that much by c. 1900 when this card was published? The two ladies standing and one seated are outside the Gelert Temperance Hotel!

THE SQUARE BEDDGELERT

BEDDGELERT, c. 1933

In 1802 the Royal Goat Hotel, seen in the distance, was built to cater for early tourists and provide quality accommodation. The Tanronen, meaning 'beneath the trees', was a much later addition. On the right is Glanafon with its gift and souvenir shop advertising Wills's Gold Flake; Goss China and Kodak Film. Ices are available further along; next door to the Tanronen Hotel they are advertising Wills's Capstan and are displaying a large selection of postcards. Oh! to be able to turn back the clock — enamel signs, collectable china and postcards — and that AA sign! Is the gentleman in uniform a chauffeur or a Crosville Motor Services inspector? There appears to be a parked charabanc in the distance.

31

LLEWELYN'S COTTAGE, c. 1905

Tradition has it that this ancient house, which stands on the southern end of the bridge across the Afon Colwyn, was the hunting lodge of Prince Llewelyn the Great, Prince of North Wales. Once known as Ty Isaf (the Lower House) it was a tavern but after various uses, including a cafe and, ownership by the Cyclists' Touring Club, it is in the hands of the National Trust, selling souvenirs and postcards etc. It is known as Llewelyn's Cottage or House.

BEDDGELERT, LLEWELYN COTTAGE.

LLEWELYN'S COTTAGE, c. 1935

A later view of Llewelyn's Cottage shows it when providing 'teas' and accommodation for members of the Cyclists' Touring Club and the Clarendon Cycling Club. The former shop of J. Williams which stood on the opposite corner is now selling Esso petrol from a manual pump. Two 1930s hikers are striding purposefully towards the bridge, the lady having just, apparently, bought something which she is carrying in her right hand. A Photochrom postcard postally used in London in August 1952, it was sent to a London address, with the message entirely in Welsh.

33

THE 'OLD' BRIDGE, BEDDGELERT, c. 1905

In this photograph, the Afon Colwyn looks calm and shallow as it drifts gently down to meet the Afon Glaslyn — a deceptive impression as local residents well know. During times of heavy rain, or melting snows, it can rise to a dangerous level, sometimes flooding properties on the river-bank. It was such an occasion, with the waters dashing along, which destroyed the bridge in 1799. Soon afterwards the stout stone bridge seen here was built. On the right is the Colwyn Temperance Hotel and, nearer the camera, The Prince Llewelyn Hotel. A ladder is visible beyond the bridge: did the photographer use this to descend — with his equipment — to the riverbed?

THE OLD BRIDGE, BEDDGELERT, c. 1930

The Glanafon Guest House lies beyond the bridge, opposite the Tanronen Hotel. Powell is the proprietor of the gift and souvenir shop in Glanafon and it is the same Powell who published a large series of postcards of the area of which there are two examples in this book. Beyond the houses lies Moel Hebog, overshadowing the village built in a valley thought to have been a lake many centuries ago. Six men stand on the bridge, one of them watching the two ladies hastily making their way from the pathway which leads from Gelert's Grave.

VIEW AT BEDDGELERT.

7083.

AFON GLASLYN, BEDDGELERT, c. 1925

Stepping stones lead across the Afon Glaslyn to the Green, but surely, in times of flood, they would be unusable and the alternative would be the old Mill footbridge about 300 yards further upstream. In the 1960s a footbridge was constructed about 100 yards upstream from the stones, ensuring a dry crossing at all times. Yr Aran is visible with the peaks of Y Lliwedd beyond and to the right.

The Old Mill and Bridge, Beddgelert.

THE OLD MILL, BEDDGELERT, c, 1902

Thomas Roscoe Esq., in his 1838 publication *Wanderings and Excursions In North Wales,* writes of his stay in Beddgelert '...and took my way towards the rude, picturesque looking mill, with its noisy steam and rock-strewn bed. Its modern use and antique appearance seem sufficiently at variance: but its lonely site, its rustic air, the dashing of its waters, with the whole scene around and beyond, are such as to arrest the eye of the painter'. The Old Mill and Bridge lay approximately 300 yards up the Afon Glaslyn from the point where it meets the Afon Conway.

SARACEN'S HEAD HOTEL, c. 1935

The old 'Ty Uchaf' (the Upper House) in Beddgelert was on the opposite side of the bridge to 'Ty Isaf', Llewelyn's Cottage. Its walls now form part of the Saracen's Head Hotel, on the Caernarfon road which is completely devoid of vehicles — in marked contrast to today. The mass of Craig-y-Llan encloses the eastern side of Beddgelert.

BEDDGELERT & SNOWDON.   7076.

BEDDGELERT, c. 1925

Where three passes meet is where Beddgelert can be found. From the north west, Nant Colwyn, through which the Afon Colwyn flows and also the line of the Roman road from Segontium to Tremadoc. The north east brings the Afon Glaslyn, by way of Llynau Gwynant and Dinas, through Nant Gwynant. The rivers meet at Beddgelert, joining forces to rush down the third pass, southwards, through the Pass of Aberglaslyn. Craig Wen, 1985 ft, is to the north with beyond, Yr Aran, 2451 ft, a satellite to Snowdon (Yr Wyddfa) being seen in the distance.

ABERGLASLYN PASS, c. 1910

Pont Aber Glaslyn, at the lower end of the Pass of Aberglaslyn, carries the A4085 away from the A498, on its way to Penrhyndeudraeth. In the eighteenth century, the bridge was at the head of the estuary and boats were built nearby, but between 1808 and 1811 the final stage in the closing off of this area from the sea was completed, the river being diverted into a purpose-built channel. The message on the card which was not postally used is 'The scenery all through this pass is very lovely and the picture does not in the least exaggerate, Bob'. I couldn't agree more.

40

ABERGLASLYN PASS, c. 1928

Sightseers on the bridge include two men sitting precariously on the wall above the signs indicating Beddgelert to the left, Penrhyndeudraeth to the right. The fingerpost bears the placenames Tremadoc and Maentwrog. To the right of the picture is an early motorcycle combination, the sidecar complete with picnic basket. The passenger in the sidecar appears to be a lady — nothing unusual about that, but, look at the rider leaning against the wall, to the rear of the combination. Yes, another lady, wearing lightweight shoes unsuited to motorcycling! An anonymous, undated card but the motorcycle is firmly dated in the 1920s.

41

LLYN DINAS, c. 1900

Llyn Dinas, through which the Afon Glaslyn flows, lies below Yr Aran in Nant Gwynant. At its southerly end can be found a mound with associations supporting the legend of King Arthur. The mound is Dinas Emrys and is connected with that great worker of magic, Merlin, and King Vortigern who held his court here. Fine trout here abounded in the lake but the increasing level of copper in the water, from the mines, soon reduced their numbers. Above the lake on its south western side is the pass leading to the old copper mine workings of the upper diggings of Sygun.

LLYN DINAS, c. 1950

Ignore the mis-spelt caption to this card. It is of course, Moel Hebog, 2566 ft high and towering over Beddgelert. Near to Moel Hebog is Moel yr Ogof, the high point to the right where, above the Beddgelert forest, can be found the cave in which Owain Glyndwr, leader of the Welsh revolt in 1400, hid when the tide had turned by 1410 and the English were again in control and the Welsh leader was a fugitive.

MOEL HEHOG & DINAS LAKE.   OS3691

43

98129 J.V.   LLYN GWYNANT, N. WALES

LLYN GWYNANT, c. 1928

Llyn Gwynant lies in Nant Gwynant and is skirted by the road between Pen-y-Gwryd and Beddgelert. It is through here that the waters of the Afon Glaslyn flow on their way from Llyn Glaslyn via the Aberglaslyn Pass and onward to Portmadoc and the sea. The high mountain is Yr Aran, 2451 ft. Imagine today's speeding motorists being confronted by a flock of sheep in the roadway. Things were very much different when this card was published in 1929 and the sender recalls, 'We stopped close by where this was taken on Monday, as you'll recognise it. The lavatory was still higher up in the valley.'

"HAFOD TAN-Y-GRAIG", NANT GWYNANT.

SNOWDON FROM NANT GWYNANT, c. 1930

Hafod Tan-y-Graig lies just below the Forestry Commission plantation, Coederyr, above Nant Gwynant. Across the pass can be seen the lower section of the Watkin Path as it makes its way past the waterfalls and into Cwm-y-Llan. Craig Ddu and Y Lliwedd rise to the right of the path and, certainly not seen from its best viewpoint, just topped by light cloud is Yr Wyddfa. Close examination will reveal the collection of 'shacks' on the Summit which indicates that, though the card is undated, the photograph was taken before 1936.

LLYN LLYDAW, c. 1905

Across Llyn Llydaw can be seen the crushing plant used for taking the metal ores, mainly copper, out of the mountain. To facilitate removal of the ore from the site the causeway was built in 1853 across the lake enabling pack horses and wagons to be used in place of boats. The mine was finally closed in 1926 but today the remains of the old buildings can still be found here with miners' barracks near Llyn Teyrn and Llyn Glaslyn.

46

LLYN LLYDAW, c. 1905

Clearly seen in this card published by Powell of Beddgelert is the Miners' Track as it climbs from the shore of Llyn Llydaw to Llyn Glaslyn. Around the corner the walker will see the continuation of the pathway as it joins The Pyg Track under Crib- y-Ddysgl. Llyn Glaslyn (the Blue Lake) probably owes its bright turquoise colour to the presence of copper but, although today it is totally unfit to drink, its old name was Llyn Ffynnon Las (the Lake of the Green Well).

SIOI. SNOWDON.   JUDGES LTD.

MINERS' TRACK, SNOWDON, c. 1910

Looking along the Miners' Track, originally laid in 1856, with Yr Wyddfa prominent in the view. Laid to enable the removal of copper ore from Snowdon, it was also used by the men from the mines to reach their barracks on the side of Llyn Teyrn (Lake of the Monarch) (King Arthur?). Copper has been mined here since Roman times. The Miners' Track is one of the most popular paths up Snowdon with an easy start but surprisingly difficult finish for the unwary.

Llanberis.

Penwgwryd Hotel.

PEN-Y-GWRYD HOTEL, c. 1900

The Pen-y-gwryd Hotel lies at the junction of the road from Capel Curig through Nant Gwryd and the road through the Llanberis Pass which had been completed in 1830. It was soon after this completion that John Roberts of Llanberis began the construction of his hotel lying to the eastern side of Snowdon, within easy access of the Snowdon Horseshoe. It has always been a favourite with walkers and climbers and was used in the early 1950s by the team, led by Colonel (later Sir) John Hunt, which succeeded in conquering Everest on 29 May 1953. Using the Pen-y-Gwryd Hotel as their base the team practised techniques in wintertime Snowdonia. Their signatures can be found in the Everest Room at the Hotel.

SNOWDON FROM NEAR PEN-Y-GWRYD, c. 1905

Prior to the opening of the road through the Llanberis Pass in 1830, now the A4086, the way was passable only on foot or horseback. Leaving Pen-y-Gwryd at around 855 ft, the road climbs over 300 ft in less than a mile to Pen-y-Pass, 1169 ft, before dropping steadily to Llanberis. Where the road can be seen to turn sharp right is Bwlch y Gwyddel, where a battle is said to have taken place between the first Celtic settlers, who later moved to Ireland, and the second wave of Celts who settled in Wales. The name of the pass here is the Pass of the Irish (Bwlch y Gwyddel). This card shows Y Lliwedd, 2947 ft, Yr Wyddfa, 3559 ft, and Crib Goch, 3021 ft. As you see, it was published by Powell of Beddgelert.

CRIB GOCH AND PEN-Y-PASS, c. 1930

The high point of the Llanberis Pass is Pen-y-Pass, at 1169 ft almost one third the height of Snowdon, which makes it an attractive starting point for those desiring not too much climbing. There is a choice of paths from this point. An easy start, to get the reluctant climber into the mood, can be found in The Miners' Track, which makes its way via the side of Llyn Teyrn, across the Causeway of Llyn Llydaw and gently up to Llyn Glaslyn. The Pyg Track ascends moderately to Bwlch y Moch (Pass of the Pig) and then under Crib Goch. Those who desire a challenge will climb Crib Goch which dominates the view in this postcard.

PEN-Y-PASS, c. 1915

It was in the middle of the nineteenth century, not long after the opening of the road through the Llanberis Pass, that a public house was opened at Pen-y-Pass. The pub was to expand to become the Gorphwysfa Hotel which was taken over by the Youth Hostel Association in 1967. This view, taken from the Miners' Track, shows the collection of buildings at Pen-y-Pass during the first half of the twentieth century.

7433. TOP OF LLANBERIS PASS. N. WALES

JUDGES' LTD

PEN-Y-PASS, c. 1910

Low cloud sweeps across the slopes of Dinas Mot and Clogwyn Mawr. The photographer is standing close to Pen-y-Pass, 1169 ft above sea level and starting point of the Pyg Track and the Miners' Track. It was here that one found the 'Gorphwysfa' (the Resting Place).

98139 J.V.   MAIDEN OF SNOWDON, LLANBERIS PASS, N. WALES

MAIDEN OF SNOWDON, c. 1925

A simple trick of the light falling on the rock formation in Clogwyn Mawr produces the phenomenon known as the Maiden of Snowdon. Her image is seen above the trees on the right of this card published by Valentine and purchased by a collector in June 1927. The author has photographed something similar in evening sunlight on Moel Siabod.

PASS OF LLANBERIS, N. WALES.

LLANBERIS PASS, 1926

In the Llanberis Pass, midway between Nant Peris and Pen-y-Pass, is a locality known as Ynys
Hettws (Hetty's Island) which is said to be the place where a woman resided for many years during
summer, in a cavity beneath a large rock. She lived here in order to tend her sheep and milk her
cows. In those days the way through the pass would have been for pedestrians, packhorses and
cattledrovers with their herds en route to market.

Llanberis, Pass of Llanberis.

LLANBERIS PASS, c. 1895

In 1884 the London and North Western Railway Company published a *Programme of Coach Tours around the Snowdon District.* Departing Chester by train at 8.40 a.m. and arriving at Llanberis at 11.50 a.m., passengers would join the coach for the 3 hour 10 minutes drive to Betws-y-Coed whence they would depart by train at 6.55 p.m. The 1st class fare which included an outside seat on the coach was 23/-.

LLANBERIS, c. 1900

The village of Llanberis takes its name from the church of St Peris which also gives the name of one of the two lakes here, Llyn Peris. Peris was an evangelist, who was sent from Rome in the sixth century to convert the wild Welsh to Christianity, and died here. Vehicles using the Llanberis Pass now avoid the village by using the by-pass. This card shows the 'new' village of Llanberis. The 'old' village, having been renamed Nant Peris, lies within the Pass itself.

DOLBADARN CASTLE, c. 1900

From the remains of Dolbadarn Castle can be obtained a fine view across Llyn Peris and up the Llanberis Pass with the Glyders rising to the left and Clogwyn Mawr and Llechog on the right. It was this location which caused the castle to be built, as the central fortress of those commanding the passes into Caernarvonshire and Anglesey. It was thought to have been built by a Welsh prince during the eighth or ninth century and was one of the major prizes, changing hands frequently during the fifteenth century war involving Owain Glyndwr. It controlled one of the major entrances to Snowdonia.

LLYN PADARN, c. 1915

The second lake at Llanberis is Llyn Padarn, taking its name from St Padarn. In the centre of the picture can be seen the ruin of Dolbadarn Castle at the lower end of the Llanberis Pass. Eons past would have seen only one lake, approximately five miles long, but over the centuries, settlement of debris brought down by the Afon Hwch has resulted in a division of the two ends of the lake. Both Llynau Padarn and Peris are at the same height above sea level.

14853. LLANBERIS. BY LLYN PADARN - JUDGES LTD

PADARN RAILWAY, NEAR LLANBERIS, c. 1930

Holidaymakers who ride on today's Llanberis Lake Railway may not realise that the route over which they travel was laid down originally around 1824 as The Padarn Railway, using horse-drawn wagons for the conveyance of slate from the Dinorwic Quarries. Laid to a unique track gauge of 4 ft, the train would carry the wagons of the Quarries' own narrow gauge system down to Port Dinorwic, the journey time, in the days of steam haulage being 40 minutes. The card shows a train carrying empty narrow-gauge wagons two abreast on its own wagons along the shore of Llyn Padarn on the return to Dinorwic.

DINORWIC RAILWAY TERMINUS, c. 1900

The terminus of The Padarn Railway where the Dinorwic Quarries' narrow gauge wagons, laden with slate, would be loaded on to the 'broad gauge' of the 'main line'. The line closed in 1963 when the slate was transferred to road transport, and the quarry itself closed six years later. Thousands of men had been employed in the quarries of Snowdonia when North Wales slate was said to 'roof the world'. The work was extremely hard and poorly paid, but the quarries made fortunes for their owners.

Labels on image: MENAI STRAITS. PARSON'S NOSE. LLYN PADARN. SLATE QUARRIES. CWM GLAS, LLANBERIS PASS. LLYN PERIS.

CWM GLAS, SNOWDON, c. 1930

The view down the Llanberis Pass from Crib Goch showing Llyn Glas in Cwm Glas. Dinorwic's slate quarries are clearly seen in this superb photograph taken on one of those rare days when it's possible to see for miles, right across Anglesey. The passengers on the ascending train, the smoke of which can be seen just to the left of centre, will indeed have their money's-worth on this day.

YR WYDDFA, c. 1930

A fine view from The Red Ridge (Crib Goch) showing clearly Yr Wyddfa and Bwlch y Saethau (the Pass of Arrows), in legend the site of the battle resulting in the deaths of King Arthur and the Welsh giant, Rhita Gawr. King Arthur's body was borne away by his soldiers, some of whom are still hiding in caves in Snowdon awaiting his return. Rhita Gawr is buried beneath Yr Wyddfa (the Great Mound). Llyn Glaslyn, source of the mighty Afon Glaslyn, lies at the bottom of the picture.

THE SUMMIT FROM CRIB-Y-DDYSGL, c. 1930

A view of Yr Wyddfa seen from the end of the Crib Goch ridge. Highest point in Wales, it is the Mecca of those who would like to reach the heights on foot. There is rivalry, in a friendly way, during the holiday season, when crowds at the top dictate a queue be formed for a chance to stand atop the summit cairn and those who have sweated and strained to reach their goal must share it with others who have simply sat back and let the train take the strain.

THE LAST MILE, SNOWDON, c. 1900

Would anyone today consider the use of a pony to convey them up Snowdon? I think not. For those who do not have the energy to take themselves, there is the railway, but now we also have the curse of the mountain-bikers tearing up the already well-worn footpaths. 'The Last Mile' seems a bit of an exaggeration since the summit is just beyond the visible peak. The pony track is now the most-used pathway to Yr Wyddfa the Llanberis Path.

SNOWDON, VIEW FROM SUMMIT

SOUTH RIDGE AND YR ARAN, c. 1920

The South Ridge route up Snowdon from the base of Yr Aran is surely one of the quickest and steepest routes to the summit. Starting from the upper reaches of Cwm y Llan, which is also passed through on the Watkin Path, it is eventually joined by the Rhyd Ddu path just below The Saddle. Finally, just before the top, the Watkin Path comes in from the right. The peak at the bottom of the ridge is Yr Aran, 2451 ft. The high peak to the right is Moel Hebog.

VIEW FROM THE SUMMIT,
c. 1935

Looking down on Yr Aran, 2451 ft, and far off in the mists, Tremadog Bay and the coast to South Wales. There is not much in the world which can exceed the pleasures of reaching the top of a mountain after a good strenuous climb, but to arrive there in clear weather and to be able to enjoy the view is the ultimate thrill on land.

VIEW FROM THE SUMMIT OF SNOWDON   SMR 2

NORTHERN VIEW FROM CRIB-Y-DDYSGL, c. 1930

Away in the distance can be seen the twin lakes at Capel Curig, Llynau Mymbyr, but most prominent in this view from Crib-y-Ddysgl is Crib Goch, (the Red Ridge), part of the Snowdon Horseshoe and a walk to be attempted only when the wind permits. To the extreme left can be seen the summit of Glyder Fach below which lies Llyn Cwm-y-Ffynnon. The second half of the Snowdon Horseshoe is via The Watkin Path and Y Lliwedd.

FROM CRIB-Y-DDYSGL LOOKING EAST, c. 1930

The Crimea Pass through which the A470 passes from the Lledr Valley to Blaenau Ffestiniog is the local name for Bwlch-y- Gorddinan and takes its name from a mid-nineteenth century inn which stood at the top of the pass. Llyn Glaslyn, gathering its waters together right under Yr Wyddfa, is the source of the Afon Glaslyn, tumbling its way via Nant Gwynant and the Aberglaslyn Pass to Porthmadog and Tremadog Bay. The Moelwyns, Bach and Mawr, overlook Tan-y-Grisiau and the Vale of Ffestiniog.

69

THE WATKIN TRACK, SNOWDON.　　　　　　　　　　　　W.1573.

THE WATKIN TRACK, c. 1930

Sir Edward Watkin, Chairman of the Metropolitan Railway, resided in a house called The Chalet, just above the road through Nant Gwynant. He was responsible for The Watkin Path, commemorating a visit to Cwm-y-Llan, through which the pathway ascends, by W.E. Gladstone in 1892, at the age of 84. The stone, from which the elderly statesmen addressed the assembled throng, is passed on the route in one of its easy stretches. Surely, one of the steepest sections, on any path, not involving scrambling, is to be found where The Watkin Path leaves Bwlch-y-Saethau to climb to join The Rhyd Ddu Path. Beyond Llyn Llydaw can be seen Moel Siabod.

THE SNOWDON MOUNTAIN RAILWAY

When the new railway line from Caernarfon to Llanberis was opened in July 1869, Sir Richard Moon, Chairman of the London and North Western Railway was present at the ceremony. His comment on looking at Snowdon was that 'the next extension must be to the top…'

The owner of the Dinorwic Slate Quarries, on the opposite side of Llyn Padarn, Mr W.A. Assheton Smith, also owned Snowdon and refused to allow any suggestion of a railway to be built on his private estate, spoiling the beauty of his mountain. If people wished to reach the summit of Snowdon they could use the rough track covering the 4½ miles to the top.

Eventually he relented and in March 1894 a syndicate was formed as the Snowdon Mountain Tramroad and Hotels Co. Ltd.

The route to the summit was surveyed by the consultant engineers, Sir Douglas and Mr Francis Fox, who had also been responsible for surveying, among other things, the Mersey Railway, opened 1886 and the Liverpool Overhead Railway, opened 1893.

Rack and pinion, devised by Dr Roman Abt of Lucerne, Switzerland, was to be the method of traction on the railway that would be uphill all the way to the top of Snowdon. Mr Assheton Smith himself cut the first sod on 15 December 1894 and work began immediately, with two major structures at Llanberis, the viaducts.

Track laying occupied 150 men for 72 days averaging 120 yards per day, completion being on 6 January 1896. Pay was 8½d per hour for masons and 5d per hour for their labourers, with a bonus as 'height money' of 2d and 1½d per hour respectively. A five-day week was worked, the first time such a contract was recorded, and the men slept where their day's work finished.

Five locomotives built by the Swiss Locomotive & Machine Works, Winterthur, Switzerland, were delivered, along with six coaches built by the Lancaster Carriage & Wagon Co., one of which was originally without a roof.

A Board of Trade Inspector certified the railway in March 1896 and the official opening ceremony took place on Easter Monday, 6 April 1896. Two trains were to travel to the top, the second with locomotive No. 1 *Ladas* (the initials of Laura Alice Duff Assheton Smith, wife of the owner of Snowdon) and two coaches. On the descent, just above Clogwyn Station, No. 1 left the track and eventually plunged down a ravine, the crew having jumped clear. Despite reassurances by the guard to remain calm, two passengers jumped from the coaches, one of them dying from injuries received. The coaches are not coupled to the locomotive and have their own independent braking system, so there was no danger of them following *Ladas*. The line was closed for a year. An investigation discovered the cause of the accident and appropriate modifications were made ensuring safe operation without the possibility of recurrence.

THE SNOWDON MOUNTAIN RAILWAY

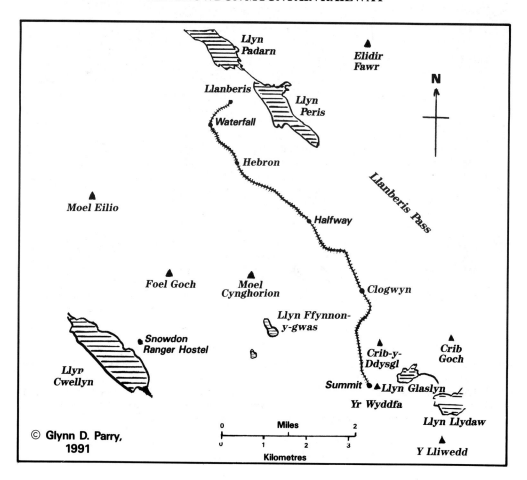

© Glynn D. Parry,
1991

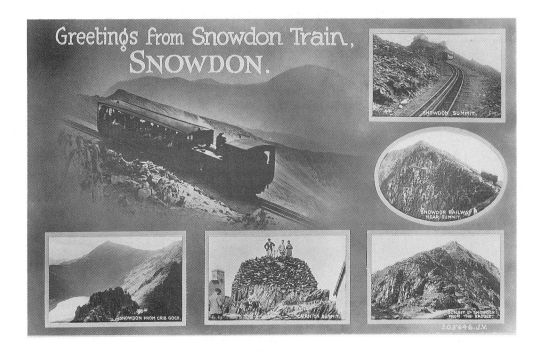

GREETINGS FROM SNOWDON TRAIN, 1933

Although this card was not published until 1933 it contains views from an earlier date. The bottom right-hand corner has the summit seen from the Saddle on the upper stretch of the South Ridge/ Rhyd Ddu/Beddgelert paths. A 'Box Brownie' is probably the camera being used to photograph the chap posing just below the cairn in the centre bottom picture. 'Snowdon Railway Near Summit' was published as a postcard on its own in 1934.

LOCOMOTIVE NO. 8, *ERYRI*

No. 8 was delivered to the Snowdon Mountain Railway Company in 1923 and remained their newest engine until the arrival of the diesels in 1986. Of the original five locomotives delivered in 1895-96 only 4 remained in service after the opening day with a further delivery of one locomotive, No. 6, in 1922 and two, Nos. 7 and 8 the following year. Notice the forward sloping boiler which, on the gradient, would be horizontal.

ON THE UPPER VIADUCT, c. 1898

Crossing the Upper Viaduct, consisting of four arches on a gradient of approximately 1 in 8½, a two-coach train, the locomotive producing very little smoke, possibly in descent. Judging by the guard's overcoat tightly fastened and the absence of leaves on the trees this must have been an early season trip — there even appears to be snow on the carriage running boards! Coaches are always propelled on ascent and held in check by the locomotive on descent, the motive power downwards being supplied by gravity.

ON THE WAY UP SNOWDON

CROSSING THE UPPER VIADUCT, c. 1916

Crossing the Upper Viaduct again, this time obviously on the ascent, with the locomotive working hard and a good number of passengers in this summertime view showing the trees bearing leaves. This card, by Dennis & Sons, was postally used in August 1916 by 'Uncle Walter' staying in Barmouth, who had just been to the summit of this beautiful mountain in the train after riding by motor and train about 50 miles through lovely mountain passes.

MOUNTAIN TRAIN ASCENDING SNOWDON

Quite clearly seen in this view is the rack designed by the Swiss engineer, Dr Roman Abt of Lucerne. The Snowdon Mountain Railway is a 'rack and pinion', meaning that traction is not by adhesion between driving wheels and running rails but is by a cogged wheel underneath the locomotive, midway between the wheels, which engages in the rack in the centre of the track.

MOUNTAIN TRAIN ASCENDING SNOWDON.

Snowdon Mountain Railway, showing Summit in distance.

SNOWDON MOUNTAIN RAILWAY SHOWING DISTANT SUMMIT

Ahead lies the summit with artist's 'snow' added. The trees are in full bloom and were the snow as heavy as this view appears to show, it is quite likely that the railway would not be operating. Hebron Station can be seen, the second station out from Llanberis, the first being Waterfall Station near Ceunant Mawr. At Hebron, named after a nearby chapel, 1 miles 8 chains out from Llanberis, the train is 950 feet up and a quarter of the way to the top.

SNOWDON RAILWAY, HALF WAY UP 706

NEAR HALFWAY STATION, c. 1920

Just below Halfway Station the railway crosses the old Pony Track, now the Llanberis Footpath. The bleakness in this view gives an indication of the task which befell the men constructing the line — in wintertime. Adding to their discomfort was the need to camp at the end of each day's labour. Raw materials, hauled up from Llanberis by horses, could take a full day to reach the working site. How many of today's railway passengers give even a passing thought to the hardships endured by the builders of Britain's only rack and pinion mountain railway?

SNOWDON RAILWAY & CLOGWYN DU'R ARDDU.   7064

TOWARDS THE SUMMIT FROM LLECHOG

The summit cannot be seen in this view showing a 'services' train below Clogwyn Station, the last station before the top, where fantastic views into the Llanberis Pass are seen. During the season that the railway operates, a train must be operated to the summit every day irrespective of the weather — this is to supply vital needs, like water, to the staff in the cafe.

Snowdon Train at Clogwyn Station

NO. 4, *SNOWDON* AT CLOGWYN STATION, 1903

In the early days of operation, the Snowdon Mountain Railway was controlled by semaphore signals, and here we see a train checked at Clogwyn Station until the descending train has passed. Following the accident on the opening day of the line, an enquiry was held and reported that No. 1 *Ladas* had left the rails following subsidence in the road bed caused by severe frost. Girders were placed on each side of the rack and grippers, fitted to the locomotives, engaged with these, thus preventing a recurrence of the mishap.

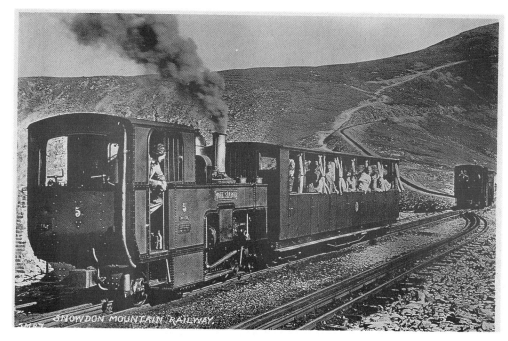

NO. 5, *MOEL SIABOD* AT CLOGWYN STATION, c. 1936

No semaphore signals visible in this view indicates that it was taken after 1930 when the old signalling system, found to be unnecessary, was dismantled. Control of the trains is now by telephone and ticket of authorisation issued to the guard of each train by a 'blockman' stationed at the passing loops at Hebron, Halfway and Clogwyn. The 'totem' carried by the coach, using a design incorporating the Welsh dragon, was introduced in 1936. The coach is one of the second batch of three received by the Railway during 1921-22 and built by the Societe Industrielle Suisse, Neuhausen. These brought the total number at that time to nine.

9005. THE TRAIN ON SNOWDON - JUDGE/CO.

ABOVE CLOGWYN STATION, c. 1918

The bridge halfway along the embankment takes the Llanberis Footpath beneath the Railway. Elidir Fawr, 3030 ft, dominates this view which also shows the upper galleries of the Dinorwic Slate Quarries. Clogwyn Station is the highest point to which trains will operate during the season when high winds prevent the crossing of the embankment. I have personally experienced winds in excess of 100 mph at this point.

NEAR THE SUMMIT, 1934

A train descending. In order to hold back the coach the locomotive is left in forward gear with steam shut off, the fire left to die down. Water is injected into the cylinders as a cooling agent, but the heat of compression turns this into steam, which is released under the control of the driver. A maximum speed of 5 mph may be reached before automatic braking, both on the locomotive and independently on the coach, comes into operation — making it impossible for any train to 'run away'. On the summit can be seen the collection of huts which were about to be replaced at the time this card was published.

SNOWDON MOUNTAIN TRAIN.

O.S.3527

NEARING SUMMIT STATION, c. 1935

The chimney cap swivelled away from the opening indicates that, despite the apparent absence of exhaust, this train is ascending. Locomotive No. 7 *Aylwin* was one of two delivered in 1923 and is seen here only a couple of hundred yards from Summit Station. The postcard was sent with love from 'Auntie Edna' and 'Uncle Leslie' to 'Dear Hugh'. The message reads: ''Isn't this a funny train. It goes ever so high up a mountain and then comes down.''

NEARING THE SUMMIT, c. 1935

Moel Eilio, 2380 ft, is prominent in the picture with Moel Cynghorion directly above the locomotive and Llyn-Ffynnon-y-Gwas in the lower reaches of Cwm Clogwyn. It is near to this part of the railway that the Snowdon Ranger Path joins the route from Llanberis with part of the path from the side of Llyn Cwellyn being seen faintly just beyond the lake. Although the locomotive cannot be positively identified, it is one of the 2 to 5 batch with a coach from the three built in 1921-33.

Snowdon Summit & Railway.

THE SUMMIT, c. 1900

Clearly showing the collection of huts which had begun to accumulate at the summit from the 1840s onwards. With the increasing popularity of mountain climbing during the nineteenth century it was an unemployed copper miner who realised that there was a possibility that walkers would require refreshment and began serving them from a stone shelter on the top. Locomotive No. 3 *Wyddfa* has been given the all clear to proceed to Summit Station.

THE SUMMIT, c. 1905

The track of The Snowdon Mountain Railway is 2 feet 7½ inches gauge and rises at a maximum gradient of 1 in 5½, even Summit Station has a gradient of 1 in 20, and throughout the entire length of the line no part of it is level. Because of this the sleepers, the centres of which are three feet apart, are firmly attached by vertical rods into concrete set into the mountain. After all, should anything slip — and it is all downhill — there would be an enormous pile of scrap metal ending up in Llanberis!

THE SUMMIT, c. 1905

The 'hotels' at the summit, opened by two gentlemen by the name of Roberts, John and William, were owned by the Victoria Hotel and the Dolbadarn Hotel, Llanberis. Overnight accommodation was available, but proved to be less than comfortable, dependent upon the number of persons requiring a bed. A train is about to depart for Llanberis, the signal having been set for departure, although the road is still indicated 'clear' for any ascending train.

THE SUMMIT OF SNOWDON.

SUMMIT AND STATION, c. 1900

Summit Station around the turn of the century. Clearly seen adjacent to the hotel is the verandah along which overnight guests on the summit could watch the sunrise, weather permitting. The station building was for the exclusive use of the railway staff and remained until the mid-1930s.

THE SUMMIT, c. 1905

If the ladies approaching the summit have climbed to the top under their own steam then they have done extremely well because, even though they are carrying walking sticks, their footwear is certainly not fit for the job. The way that they are holding their hats would indicate that the wind is blowing quite strongly. The building adjacent to the verandah bears a board proclaiming it as the Snowdon Summit Hotel. Already quite a number of passengers are aboard the train for the descent.

THE NEW HOTEL, SNOWDON SUMMIT, c. 1936

By 1936 all of the wooden structures had gone from the summit, having been pushed down into the valley. The reason was the building of a brand new hotel and cafe incorporating the station. Designed by Clough Williams-Ellis, master-mind behind Portmeirion, the new building was completed in 1935, replacing the untidy jumble previously found at the top. No. 2 *Enid*, named after the daughter of Assheton Smith, has just left Summit Station en route for Llanberis, almost one hour away.

HOTEL AND STATION, SNOWDON SUMMIT.   W. 1574.

HOTEL AND STATION, c. 1937

The 'new' station at the summit with two trains enjoying the half hour rest between ascent and descent. No. 2 *Enid* is at the right-hand platform with No. 5 *Moel Siabod* opposite. The hotel continued to function as such until it was occupied by the Ministry of Supply and later the Air Ministry from 1942 to 1945, when experimental radio and radar work was carried out. The Navy and the Army were also 'in occupation'. Accommodation since has been only for cafe staff who are here during the railway season.

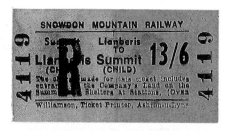

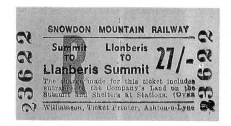

SNOWDON MOUNTAIN RAILWAY TICKETS

A small selection of Snowdon Mountain Railway tickets bearing a reminder of pre-decimal currency, when 240 pennies made a pound and prices above £1 were frequently quoted in shillings. (The author would be grateful to hear from readers who may own earlier examples).

Single circle, 25mm
blue ink
pre-1914

Double circle, 37mm
purple ink
1920s

Single circle, 22mm
purple, red or black ink
1930s

Single circle, 32mm
purple or black ink, 1950s
(a later version measures 35mm, 1970s)

Single circle, 23mm, bilingual
black ink, 1980s,
applied with Railway letter stamp
(depicting Afon Hwch viaduct)
introduced late 1980s

SUMMIT OF SNOWDON CACHETS

One of the attractions of buying postcards at the summit was that, not only could they be endorsed with a rubber stamp (cachet), but really could be posted there. A special train known as 'The Mail' had run since the early days of the railway when souvenir postcards were carried non-stop to Llanberis. Mail is now carried on the ordinary trains and there is a supplementary railway letter stamp which covers the cost of transport.

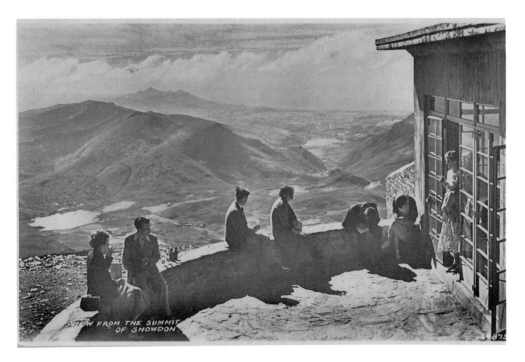

VIEW FROM THE SUMMIT, c. 1937

Sitting outside the hotel writing 'wish you were here...' cards. In this remarkably clear view can
be seen: Y Garn and the Nantlle Ridge; Yr Eifel at the head of the Lleyn Peninsula; Llyn y Gadair;
Llyn y Dywarchen and Llyn Nantlle Uchaf. The large windows of the hotel were blown in within
six months of opening in 1936 and were replaced by smaller ones.

NOTES FOR VISITORS TO SNOWDONIA

You have now had a taste of the magnificence of Snowdon, albeit that of the past. The magnificence remains, as do the dangers.

Tens, perhaps hundreds of thousands each year attempt the climb to the top, but Snowdon and all its neighbours still demand respect. If you are tempted to try the climb, remember the following points:

If in any doubt about your fitness to do it — don't.

If possible, tell someone where you are going, and what time you expect to return.

Footwear and clothing are very important. Stout waterproof boots are essential for the rough tracks you may use. The weather can change very rapidly, even on the best summer days, and the higher you climb the colder it gets, so always carry warm clothing with you.

Study the weather forecast charts found at the start of each of the popular Snowdon paths, and remember forecasts can be wrong. Sudden local changes can occur right where you are.

Always stick to the path — don't wander about the mountain.

Take food and drink with you in case of unexpected prolonged stays.

If you find it difficult to use common sense, but still want to reach the highest summit in Wales, then use the railway.

However, if you come to enjoy the beauty of Snowdonia, please remember:

Take nothing but photographs; leave nothing but footprints

Local titles published by S.B. Publications in the series 'A Portrait in Old Picture Postcards'

Bootle, Vols 1 & 2	Aberystwyth
Liverpool, Vols 1 & 2	
Rock Ferry, New Ferry and Bebington	Bangor
Old Bebington	Llandudno
Southport	
	Rhyl
Chester, Vols 1 & 2	Denbigh
The Villages of Cheshire	Ruthin and District
Crewe	Wrexham and District
	Connah's Quay
Bury	Hawarden
The Bridgewater Canal	Llangollen
The Manchester Ship Canal	Chirk and the Glyn Valley Tramway
The lost villages of Manchester	Chirk
Bournville	Oswestry and District
The Black Country, Vols 1 & 2	Shrewsbury
Wolverhampton, Vols 1 & 2	Bridgnorth
Stourbridge and District	Wellington

Liverpool to North Wales pleasure-steamers
The Blue Funnel Line
Constabulary Duties: A History of Policing

Other local titles available and in preparation for full details write to S.B. Publications, Unit 2, The Old Station Yard, Pipe Gate, Market Drayton, Shropshire TF9 4HY (please enclose SAE).